EXPLORING THE WORLD

MARCO POLO

Marco Polo and the Silk Road to China

BY MICHAEL BURGAN

Content Adviser: Heather Clydesdale, former Assistant Director for Curriculum Development, Asia Society, and Ph.D. candidate in Chinese Art History, Columbia University

Social Science Adviser: Professor Sherry L. Field, Department of Curriculum and Instruction, College of Education, The University of Texas at Austin

Reading Adviser: Dr. Linda D. Labbo, Department of Reading Education, College of Education, The University of Georgia

COMPASS POINT BOOKS
MINNEAPOLIS, MINNESOTA

Compass Point Books
3722 West 50th Street, #115
Minneapolis, MN 55410

Visit Compass Point Books on the Internet at *www.compasspointbooks.com* or
e-mail your request to *custserv@compasspointbooks.com*

Photographs ©: North Wind Picture Archives, cover, back cover (background), 1, 2 (background), 4, 8,
24, 31, 34 (all), 35, 46–47 (background); Hulton Getty/Archive Photos, 6, 19, 25; Historical Picture
Archive/Corbis, 7; Adam Woolfitt/Corbis, 9, 21; Stock Montage, 10, 11, 12, 17, 32, 37, 38; Keren
Su/Corbis, 13; Bettmann/Corbis, 15, 26; Art Resource, N.Y., 16; Giraudon/Art Resource, N.Y., 20, 27,
39; Corbis, 22; Dean Conger/Corbis, 24; Bohemian Nomad Picturemakers/Corbis, 28; Sheldan
Collins/Corbis, 29; Ric Ergenbright/Corbis, 30; SEF/Art Resource, N.Y., 41.

Editors: E. Russell Primm, Emily J. Dolbear, and Melissa McDaniel
Photo Researchers: Svetlana Zhurkina and Jo Miller
Photo Selector: Catherine Neitge
Designer: Design Lab, Inc.
Cartographer: XNR Productions, Inc.

Library of Congress Cataloging-in-Publication Data
Burgan, Michael.
    Marco Polo : Marco Polo and the silk road to China / by Michael Burgan.
      p. cm. — (Exploring the world)
    Includes bibliographical references (p.   ).
    Summary: A biography of the thirteenth-century Venetian explorer whose book about his travels
across Asia and work for Kubla Khan helped to launch the Age of Exploration.
    ISBN 0-7565-0180-6 (hardcover)
    1. Polo, Marco, 1245–1323?—Journeys—Juvenile literature. 2. Explorers—Italy—Biography—
Juvenile literature. 3. Travel, Medieval—Juvenile literature. 4. Asia—Description and travel—Juvenile
literature. [1. Polo, Marco, 1245–1323? 2. Explorers. 3. Voyages and travels. 4. Asia—Description and
travel.] I. Title. II. Series.
  G370.P9 B844 2002
  915.04'2'092—dc21   2001004731

Printed in the United States of America.

Table of Contents

Explorer of Asia

In a jail in Genoa, Italy, a prisoner told a fantastic tale. The man talked of his travels in distant lands and the people who lived there. The traveler had spent many years working for Kublai Khan, a great ruler. And now he wanted his cellmate, a writer named Rustichello, to write down his tale. The traveler who had seen and heard so many wondrous things was Marco Polo.

The story Marco Polo told Rustichello is known today as *Description of the World*, though some people call it *The Travels of*

This portrait of Marco Polo was first done in mosaic by Francesco Salviati in the 1500s.

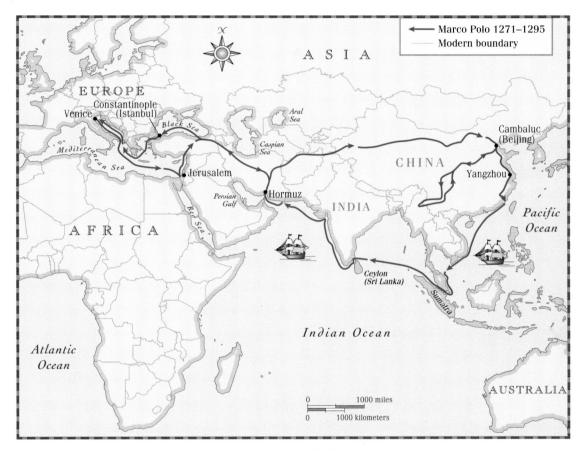

A map of Marco Polo's travels

Marco Polo. Written in 1298, the book gave many Europeans their first glimpse of lands they knew almost nothing about. Marco's story made people curious about Asia and its riches. Less than two hundred years later, when explorer Chris-

Marco Polo is shown dictating his story to Rustichello on the cover of a book by Sir Henry Yule published in London in 1874.

topher Columbus sailed west looking for a route to Asia, he took Marco's book with him.

Marco did not actually see everything described in his book. Other people told him about some of the places and things he mentioned. Nor did Marco always note when or where things happened. And, as Rustichello points out, Marco told "only what little he was able to remember." But the tale of his adventures shows readers how people lived in Asia during the thirteenth century.

A City—and Family—of Traders

Marco Polo was born in 1254, most likely on the island of Korcula, in the Adriatic Sea. This island was controlled by Venice, a series of islands in the shallow water near the Adriatic on the east coast of Italy. The city is famous for its canals—small waterways that link the islands.

This painting by nineteenth-century artist Giovanni Battista Borghese shows the Rialto Bridge and the Grand Canal in Venice.

In Marco's time, Venice was an important trading center. Merchants from all over Europe went there to sell furs, lumber, metal, and slaves. Traders from the Middle East and other parts of Asia brought spices, gems, and other expensive items. By 1200, Venice was one of the largest and richest cities in Europe.

Marco's father, Nicolo, was a successful businessman. He and his brother Maffeo traded in Venice and then in Constantinople (now called Istanbul) in Turkey. Nicolo and Maffeo left for Constantinople just before Marco was born. The Polo brothers did well there, but they

Constantinople in the early 1300s

were tempted by the money they could make elsewhere. In 1260, they left Constantinople for the Crimea, a region that borders the Black Sea in what is now the Ukraine. As Marco later learned, however, his father and uncle went far beyond the Crimea.

The Polo brothers traveled and traded for many years. Meanwhile, back in Venice, Marco's mother died, and he was raised by relatives. Marco was fifteen years old when he saw his father for the first time. Nicolo and Maffeo had returned with great stories—and as friends of the world's most powerful ruler.

The birthplace of Marco Polo in Venice

Into Mongol Lands

In his book, Marco also describes some of his father's adventures. After leaving the Crimea, the Polo brothers continued east. They eventually came to lands controlled by Barka Khan. He was one of the Mongols who ruled most of Asia at this time.

A few centuries earlier, the

An old Chinese drawing shows a Mongol caravan on the way to Beijing.

Mongols had been tribes of **nomads** scattered around central Asia, north and west of China. They lived in felt tents called yurts and rode small, powerful horses. At the end of the 1100s, the Mongol tribes united to fight neighboring peoples. Skilled warriors on horseback, the Mongols easily defeated their enemies. Under their great leader Genghis Khan, the Mongols swept across China and into Russia. Finally they reached Europe, invading Hungary and Poland in 1241. After that, the Mongols **retreated** to Asia.

Barka Khan, a grandson of Genghis, welcomed the Polos and traded with them. They stayed with Barka for a year. When they were ready to return to the

Kublai Khan on his throne

Crimea, a war blocked their path. So Nicolo and Maffeo continued traveling east. They crossed a desert before reaching the city of Bukhara, a major trading center. The brothers stayed there for three years. Then, in 1265, they received an invitation to meet the most important Mongol ruler of the time—Kublai Khan.

The Polo brothers entering the gates of Bukhara,
where they stayed for three years

Kublai ruled China and other parts of eastern Asia. He was both a great general in wartime and a wise leader in peacetime. He welcomed traders from many lands. Marco writes that Nicolo and Maffeo Polo were told that Kublai would treat them with "great honor and great **bounty**." The Polos gladly went to meet the man called the Great Khan.

Contact Between Asia and Western Europe

Before the Polos' trip across Asia, few Europeans had visited China. Most trade between Europe and China was done by land, with traders from the Middle East and Persia (now Iran) doing most of the work.

They traveled on transcontinental trade routes, known today as The Silk Roads.

Some Christians also traveled east, hoping to bring their religion to Asia and establish diplomatic ties with the power-

A camel caravan travels along China's Silk Road today.

ful Mongols. A missionary named John Pian di Carpini reached Mongol lands in 1246. Another, William of Rubruck, arrived in 1254. He saw several other Europeans there working for the Mongols. Genghis Khan and the Mongols were tolerant of other religions and cultures. They knew they could not keep their power over their huge empire if they weren't.

But for the most part, Europe was cut off from Asia. After the Roman Empire crumbled in the fifth century, Europe entered what is now called the Dark Ages. Education was ignored, most people were poor, and invaders from the east attacked often. To the south, along the Mediterranean Sea,

Arab states rose to power. Most of the Arabs were Muslims—followers of the faith of Islam. They sometimes clashed with the Christians in parts of Europe and the Middle East. The Arab states controlled travel and trade to Asia. In Polo's time, European countries were still rebuilding their strength.

When the Polo brothers arrived in China, Kublai is said to have greeted them warmly and asked many questions about Europe. According to Marco Polo, he also gave the brothers a message for the pope, the head of the Roman Catholic Church. The Great Khan wanted the pope to send 100 religious **scholars** to his court. They were to explain to Kublai why they

Kublai Khan greeting the Polo brothers, as shown in this fourteenth-century drawing

believed Christianity was better than other religions.

Kublai also asked the Polos to do him a special favor. He wanted them to return with oil from the lamp that burned at the Holy Sepulcher in Jerusalem, in present-day Israel. According to Christians, Jesus was buried on this spot.

Oil from the lamp there was said to have healing powers.

The Polos agreed. They left for Europe, traveling with a Mongol **baron**. The three men carried a gold tablet signed by Kublai. The tablet told anyone who met the travelers that they **represented** Kublai Khan. It **guaranteed** them a safe trip.

Kublai Khan gave his golden seal to the Polo brothers. From Le Livre des Merveilles, *a fourteenth-century illuminated manuscript that describes the travels of the Polos and others.*

now in Israel, they learned that the pope had just died. The Polos decided to return to Venice until a new pope was elected. There Nicolo saw his son Marco for the first time. Nicolo and Maffeo spent two years in

The baron became sick along the way, so he stayed behind. Nicolo and Maffeo continued on. When they reached Acre, a city then in Syria and Venice waiting for a new pope to come to power. Finally, in 1271, the Polo brothers prepared to return to China. This time, they took Marco along.

Marco Polo's house in Venice

Marco's Adventure Begins

Marco, now seventeen years old, sailed with his father and uncle to Acre. The journey was difficult. European ships in the thirteenth century were often crowded and dirty. Rats and cockroaches scampered around, and the water onboard was sometimes barely drinkable.

The trip to Acre took a little more than a month. From there, the Polos traveled to Jerusalem to get the lamp oil for Kublai Khan. They returned to Acre, then set off for China, even though they did not have the 100 scholars Kublai had requested. A new pope had not been chosen either, but the Polos did not want to wait any longer.

They headed north. After only a few days of travel, they learned that the Roman Catholic Church had finally chosen a new pope—Gregory X. The Polos had already met Pope Gregory in Acre. They now returned there to receive his blessing for their trip.

Gregory was not ready to send 100 scholars to China. But as Marco writes, the pope "sent the Great Khan many gifts, fine **vessels** of crystal and other things." He also had two **friars**

The Polos are shown leaving Venice in this illustration from a fourteenth-century manuscript in the Bodleian Library in Oxford, England.

travel with the Polos. These religious men would try to persuade the people they met to become Christians.

The friars did not last long. Soon after the travelers left Acre, they stumbled into a war. The frightened friars decided to return to Acre and the Polos continued the trip on their own.

The Polo brothers met with Pope Gregory X, from Le Livre des Merveilles.

Through the Middle East and Beyond

The Polos traveled through Turkey, Armenia, and Iraq. They saw Mount Ararat, where some people believed Noah's Ark was buried in the snow. Marco also saw "a spring from which gushes a stream of oil." The oil, he says, is "good for burning." This oil was petroleum, which is used today to make gasoline, chemicals, and other products. It is

Mount Ararat

Kublai Khan is shown in battle. The Mongols controlled all the lands the Polos visited.

the chief product traded along The Silk Roads today.

The Mongols controlled all the lands the Polos visited. If not for the Mongols, Marco writes, the local people "would do great mischief to traveling merchants." Even the power of the Mongols was not always enough to prevent crime, though. On his journey, Marco "narrowly evaded capture by . . . robbers in the darkness." Others traveling with the Polos were not so lucky. "Many . . . were taken captive and sold, and some put to death," Marco writes.

The Polos finally reached the city of Hormuz on the Persian Gulf. They planned to sail on to China, but they changed their minds when they saw the boats used on the Indian Ocean. The ships were held together with wooden pegs and thread—not with the iron nails used in Europe. "And you can take my word that many of them sink," Marco writes, "because the Indian Ocean is often very stormy."

The Polos continued their journey by land. They traveled across deserts and over mountains. At times, they passed through lands filled with fruit trees and animals. They crossed northern Afghanistan, where Marco learned of great mines filled with silver and valuable gems, such as rubies.

In this region, Marco fell ill—some sources say he was

Sand dunes along the edge of the Gobi Desert

ill for up to a year. He finally recovered in the fresh mountain air, and the Polos continued their trip. They again crossed deserts, including the vast Gobi in China. Marco says that travelers on the Gobi sometimes heard "spirit voices," music, and other strange sounds. The voices, Marco says, tricked travelers into leaving their path and getting lost.

When the Polos neared the Great Khan, he sent men to greet them. Marco writes that Kublai "received them honorably and entertained them with good cheer." It had taken Marco, Nicolo, and Maffeo more than three years to reach the Mongol leader. They had traveled across deserts, through snowstorms, and over flooded rivers. Marco had seen things few other Europeans had ever seen. And his travels were just beginning.

The Polos are shown with their caravan in this old illustration.

Servant of the Great Khan

In his book, Marco describes Kublai Khan "as the greatest lord the world has ever known." During the winter, Kublai lived in a palace in Cambaluc (now Beijing, China). Marco was impressed with the palace, which was surrounded by walls 4 miles (6.4 kilometers) long. "Inside," Marco says, "the walls

Kublai Khan greets Marco Polo in this miniature painting from Le Livre des Merveilles.

of the halls and chambers are covered with gold and silver and decorated with pictures of dragons and birds and horsemen . . . and scenes of battle." Kublai had riches from throughout his kingdom brought to Cambaluc. "The Great Khan must have . . . more treasure than any-one else in the world," Marco wrote.

Marco also told of how the Mongols used paper money, something Europeans had never seen. Paper itself was still rare in parts of Europe, but the Chinese had been using it for more than 1,000 years.

Marco Polo, as shown in a painting from the Museo Correr in Venice

The Polos were lucky to be the guests of such a powerful host. Marco was also given another honor. The Kublai Khan sent him across his lands as his **representative**. Marco had already learned the Mongol language and probably also spoke Persian, Turkish, and Arabic. These languages were helpful, because people from all over Asia lived in and traded with the Mongol **empire**.

Marco spent time on the east coast of China, in the city of Yangzhou. Marco claimed that he was governor of the city for three years, but Chinese records do not list his name. Some historians believe he may

A stone footbridge arches over a lake in modern-day Yangzhou.

have held a less impor-
tant government posi-
tion there.

Throughout his
book, Marco also
describes places out-
side of China, including
Burma (now called
Myanmar), Japan,
India, and Tibet. He
notes the different reli-
gions people followed
in these areas, such as
Buddhism and Hinduism.

A man pans for rubies, sapphires, and other gems in modern-day Sri Lanka.

He also describes what people
ate. The Indians, he writes, ate
plenty of rice and refused to
eat beef. In one part of India,
the people pulled bark off the
sago tree and made a kind of
flour from the insides. "It is
then seasoned and made into
cakes and various paste dishes,
which are exceedingly good."

Marco was also impressed
by the goods the people traded.
As the son of a merchant, he
was particularly interested in
Asia's riches. In Ceylon (now
Sri Lanka) he saw rubies,

sapphires, and other gems. The Japanese, he said, have gold and pearls. He saw cotton, leather, and "cushions stitched with gold."

Polo also saw spices, which were highly valued in Europe. Parts of India had a lot of "pepper and also ginger, besides cinnamon in plenty and other spices." The Asian spices did not grow in Europe, and they were expensive to buy. After Marco Polo's death, the major European countries sometimes fought Asians—or each other—for the right to buy and sell these spices.

A spice merchant in modern-day India sits amid his pots of spices.

Going Home

Marco, Nicolo, and Maffeo Polo lived in Asia for more than fifteen years. The elder Polos stayed at Kublai Khan's court most of this time. They became rich by trading in jewels and

An old print shows Marco Polo and Kublai Khan traveling on the backs of elephants.

Marco Polo landed in Hormuz in the Persian Gulf. Only eighteen passengers survived the dangerous trip, from Le Livre des Merveilles.

gold. Still, they often thought about returning to Venice. They asked the Great Khan if they could go home. "But he . . . so much enjoyed their company," Marco writes, "that nothing would induce him to give them leave."

Finally, in 1292, Kublai Khan allowed the Polos to leave. They left China with three Mongols who were traveling to Persia to bring a new bride to one of Kublai's nephews. Before the Polos left, the Great Khan gave them two gold tablets. He also sent messages to the pope and European leaders.

A party of thirteen ships left for Persia carrying 600 passengers. By the time the ships reached the port of Hormuz in Persia nearly two years later, only eighteen passengers were still alive. The Polos were among the few who survived that long, dangerous voyage.

From Persia the Polos headed west overland until they reached Trebizond, on the Black Sea. From there they sailed to Constantinople and then home to Venice. It was 1295, and Marco had been away for twenty-four years.

Soldier, Prisoner, Merchant

Venice did not welcome the Polos as heroes. No one even seemed to know much about their trip. Nicolo and Maffeo used part of their wealth to buy a new house. Marco later lived there, too. He also set off on another adventure, as a sailor in Venice's navy.

The cities of Venice and

Medallions of Marco Polo and Kublai Khan

A print of Marco Polo's ship in battle was used in Sir Henry Yule's The Book of Ser Marco Polo.

Genoa were battling for control of trade in the region. In about 1296, Marco was serving on a ship in the Adriatic Sea. During one battle, Genoese ships defeated a Venetian **fleet** and Marco was taken prisoner. It was during his time in jail that Marco met Rustichello and dictated *Description of the World.*

Historians do not know much about Marco's life after he left prison. He certainly lived in Venice as a trader. He earned the nickname *Il Milione*, meaning "the Millions." Some people say this is because he always talked about the millions of coins owned by the Great Khan. When he died in 1324, he left behind a wife and three daughters.

Marco Polo Today

Many questions remain about Marco Polo and his travels. His book appeared in several different versions. In the fourteenth century, books were copied by hand.

Not every copy of Marco's book had the same facts. Historians also know Marco made up some of the things he claimed. He says he saw unicorns, and he describes

Marco Polo claimed to have seen unicorns and other mythical creatures.

An engraving of Marco Polo was published in 1477.

how the Polos helped the Mongols win a battle. In fact, the battle he mentions took place before Marco ever reached the court of Kublai Khan.

Rustichello might have also changed some of Marco's words. He may have added details to make the book more exciting. Other writers also added parts to Marco's story. Some people claimed Marco introduced two treats to Europe from China—pasta and ice cream. Recent studies, however, show that Marco probably did not bring these foods to Europe.

A fresco portrait of Marco Polo from the 1500s

A few historians have suggested that Marco Polo never visited China at all. They wonder why Marco did not mention tea, which was popular in parts of China, and calligraphy, a special style of writing used on Chinese documents. Marco's doubters also note that he is not mentioned in records of the Mongol government. They point out that he could have learned about China from other travelers, especially Arab and Persian traders. Most people, however, believe Marco went to China, since he describes so many things that were true.

Even if Marco did not go to China, his book had a lasting effect on Europe. *Description of the World* appeared in many languages. It showed readers life in distant lands. Marco also pointed out China's wealth and the many ways in which China was more advanced than Europe. Most importantly, Marco inspired others to explore the world far beyond Europe and the Middle East. Marco Polo showed how much people can learn when they travel and open their eyes—and minds—to new things.

A tea shop, as shown on a 500-year-old Chinese porcelain vase. Some historians wonder why Marco Polo did not mention tea in his stories.

Glossary

baron a member of the ruling class

bounty something given generously

empire a group of countries that have the same ruler

fleet a group of ships

friar a member of a religious group

guaranteed made sure of

nomads people who wander from place to place with their animals

representative a person who acts for someone else

retreat withdraw

scholars experts in a certain field

vessel a container

Did You Know?

- Marco Polo's book *Description of the World* appears in 140 different manuscript versions, in 12 languages and dialects.

- During his travels, Marco Polo was probably the first European to see eyeglasses, ice cream, fireworks, and spaghetti!

- Just before he died, a priest tried to get Marco Polo to admit that his stories were not true. Marco responded by saying, "I did not tell half of what I saw, because no one would have believed me."

Important Dates in Marco Polo's Life

1254

Marco Polo born in Venice

1260

Nicolo and Maffeo Polo leave Constantinople and travel east

1266?

The Polos reach the court of Kublai Khan, stay for a short period, then begin their return trip

1269

The Polos arrive in Venice

1271

Marco leaves for China with his father and uncle

1275

The Polos arrive at Kublai Khan's court; Marco travels across the Mongol Empire for the next seventeen years

1292

The Polos leave China, traveling by sea.

1295

The Polos return to Venice

1296?

Marco is taken prisoner and sent to Genoa

1298

Marco and Rustichello write Description of the World

1324

Marco dies in Venice

Important People

CHRISTOPHER COLUMBUS (1451–1506) in 1492 became the first explorer to reach the Americas

GENGHIS KHAN (1162?–1227) Mongol conqueror of China, Russia, and the Middle East

KUBLAI KHAN (1215–1294) Mongol ruler of China; grandson of Genghis

MAFFEO POLO (?) trader; Nicolo's brother and Marco's uncle

NICOLO POLO (?–1299) wealthy businessman and trader; Marco's father

RUSTICHELLO OF PISA (?) Italian writer of *Description of the World*

Want to Know More?

At the Library

Dramer, Kim. *Kublai Khan.* New York: Chelsea House, 1990.

Ganeri, Anita. *Marco Polo.* Mankato, Minn.: Thameside Press, 1999.

Hull, Mary. *The Mongol Empire.* San Diego: Lucent Books, 1998.

MacDonald, Fiona. *Marco Polo: A Journey Through China.* New York: Franklin Watts, 1998.

Ventura, Piero. *Venice: Birth of a City.* Translated by John Grisewood. New York: Putnam, 1998.

On the Web

Marco Polo
http://www.geocities.com/TimesSquare/Maze/5099/sld001.html
For a slide show about the life of Marco Polo

Marco Polo and Korcula
http://www.korcula.net/mpolo/
To learn more about the life of Marco Polo

Through the Mail

The Silk Road Foundation
P.O. Box 2275
Saratoga, California 95070
To receive information on speakers and
presentations about Marco Polo

On the Road

Minneapolis Institute of Art
2400 Third Avenue South
Minneapolis, Minnesota 55404
To see a collection of Asian art that contains art
from seventeen cultures and spans 5,000 years

Index

About the Author

Michael Burgan is a freelance writer for children and adults. A history graduate of the University of Connecticut, he has written more than thirty fiction and nonfiction children's books for various publishers. For adult audiences, he has written news articles, essays, and plays. Michael Burgan is a recipient of an Edpress Award and belongs to the Society of Children's Book Writers and Illustrators.

Just last week, very early,
tooth fairies fluttered high over the city.

No one looked up. No one saw the Underhills.
Esme pushed her glasses back on her nose.
"I just LOVE sleepovers at Grandma and Grandad's," she said.
"THERE THEY ARE!" shouted her big sister, April.

Ariel the dog's tail wagged, and their wings
shivered in the wind as they
headed down.

For Silah

First U.S. edition 2019
First published by Walker Books Ltd. (U.K.) 2019

Library of Congress Catalog Card Number 2019939261
ISBN 978-1-5362-1112-2

CCP 24 23 22 21 20 19
10 9 8 7 6 5 4 3 2 1

Printed in Shenzhen, Guangdong, China

This book was typeset in Poliphilus and Blado MT.
The illustrations were done in ink and watercolor.

Candlewick Press
99 Dover Street
Somerville, Massachusetts 02144

visit us at www.candlewick.com

BOB GRAHAM

The Underhills

A Tooth Fairy Story

CANDLEWICK PRESS

There were hugs. There were kisses.
"Mommy and Daddy have to work," said Esme.
  Their new brother, Vincent, said nothing.
  He couldn't talk yet.
"Urgent molar pickup on Main Street,"
  Dad and Mom said together, then laughed.
  Dad's arm around Mom made a soft crackle of wings.

April cleared her throat and stepped forward.
"Some tadpoles for you, Grandma," she said.
"Got them from the pond.
Cute, aren't they?"

"Oh, thank you, April and Esme.
And I see an ice-pop stick floating on top."
"To sit on when they turn into frogs," said Esme.
"That's very thoughtful," replied Grandma.

"Vincent's mashed mulberries and diapers are
  in the bag, and treats for Ariel, too," called Mom.
"And our pajamas," said Esme.
"And our books and toothbrushes," added April.

"Thanks for looking after them, Grandma and Grandad,"
shouted Mom and Dad. "We'll call or text. Must fly."
But their voices were drowned in sound.

Grandma and Grandad's!
A whole day and night.
Where the tea is always hot,
there's a bed of feathers for weary wings,
and pancakes with syrup for breakfast.

On each of their pillows, April and Esme
would find a chocolate waiting for them.
"Grandma things!" they called them.

And always special was the mixing of the batter for fairy cakes . . .

and, while they cooked, the tasting of the leftover chocolate.

And then there was Grandad,
working on the heavy bag
to keep in shape.

"Just whack it, Esme!" said Grandad. "Give it all you've got."
"I am, Grandad. I am!"
Then Grandma's phone rang.

"Who's that?
Oh! Hello, Fay
darling. I'll put
you on speaker."

Then Mom spoke. "A job just came in.
Small girl. Red coat. Arriving on
flight 417 from Ghana. Name of Akuba.
Baby tooth out. Somewhere in the pocket."

"Can *we* do it, Mommy? Can *we* get the tooth?"
There was a pause. "Well . . . be careful," said Mom.
"And remember," said Dad, "Akuba must never see you.
You are spirits of the air."

"YESSS!"

And there was a small flurry of airy excitement
in that teapot house by the airport fence.

Vincent's head was heavy with sleep,
so Grandad remained behind.

Grandad tied them together so that if he should fall asleep,
too, Vincent would not float off like a balloon.
Grandad settled down with his book,
A Poem for Every Day of the Year.

"Don't need your phones, kids," he said.
"There's a big chunk of life to see out there."
With still-warm cakes in Grandma's bag,
they flew over the fence.

A huge jet shrieked overhead.

"No higher than the wire," yelled Grandma.

"Is Akuba from Ghana up there?" shouted April.

Grandma looked at her watch. "Not yet, but soon," she said.
"At the . . . the . . . terminable, Grandma?" said Esme.
"Yes, Esme, at the *terminal*."

"OH, GRANDMA!"

Down below in the terminal there was baggage,
noise, excitement, and emotion overflowing.
And, up above, only the soft beating of wings.

"I can't see Akuba," said April, as the sisters bumped across the ceiling.
"In a little while she'll be here," said Grandma.
"Let's wait over there," said Esme, "with the angels and the cupids."

"Brought your grandchildren today, Ophelia?" said an angel.
"Yes, this is April and this is Esme," replied Grandma. "This is
   Beatrice, children. And these are Apollo and Mercury, the cupids."
"Pleased to meet you," said April and Esme.

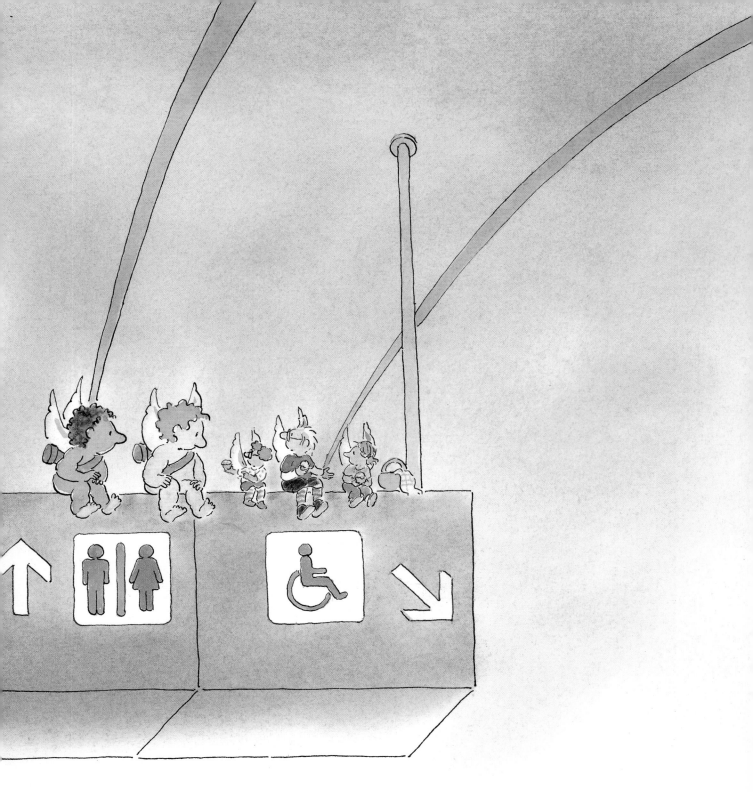

"Shouldn't the cupids have bows and arrows, Grandma?"
whispered April.
"They have to leave them at the door," said Grandma. "Security!"
"Would you like a fairy cake?" asked Esme. "Grandma made them."

"Are you waiting for Akuba, too?" Esme asked Mercury.

"Hmm! Nice cake. Who's Akuba?" he said.

"Little girl, red coat, baby tooth," said April.

"We don't do teeth," he said. "We cupids like to,
  well, just help people meet, I guess."

"And the angels?
They do the sad arrivals."

"And sometimes," Apollo added, "we just watch over."

"And the angels help push the trolleys."

Then came the announcement:

FLIGHT 417 FROM GHANA HAS LANDED.

"IT'S AKUBA! IT'S AKUBA!"
And the Underhill sisters did cartwheels of excitement.

"Grandma, Grandma, we have no coin
to give Akuba for her tooth!"
Grandma's hands flew to her face with shock.

"Oh, my dears! I forgot
to bring one," said Grandma.
"Wait! Check the vending
machines down below."

And both girls launched
themselves into the air.

They hovered in front of the vending machines,
their wings beating like small hummingbirds.

"I've *found* one, April.
Help me!"

"And . . . and . . .
THERE SHE IS!"

"But where's the tooth, April?"
"In her pocket, Esme."
"Well, which pocket?" cried Esme.
"Try the right one," called April
   as they tumbled down,
      their fingers tight on the coin.

April grabbed for the pocket
and hung on fast as Esme
swung from the coin with
her eyes shut tight.

And they crawled inside.

Deep inside the pocket,
April shouted, "HERE IT IS!"
"Shhh!" replied Esme.
"Oh, I think she heard us."
Akuba stopped and looked around.

"Quick, we have to leave," said April.
  And with the coin in Akuba's pocket and April's arms around
  the tooth, Esme whispered in Akuba's ear,
"You heard nothing, Akuba. We are spirits of the air."
  As April and Esme returned to Grandma with the tooth,
  Akuba scratched her ear once and hurried to her mom.

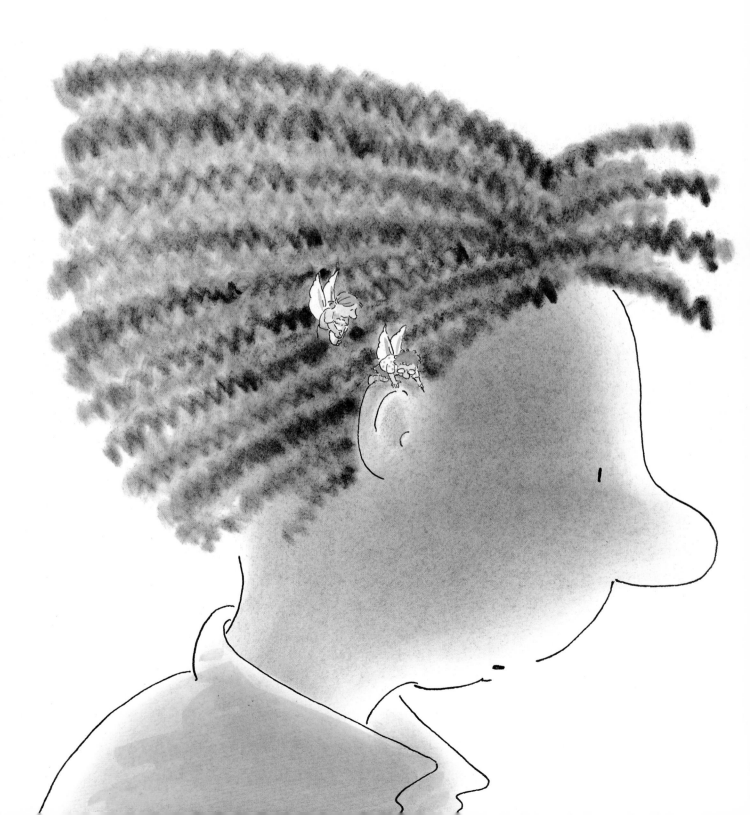

High up on the sign, Grandma was waiting.
"Grandma, Esme found a coin . . ."

"And we found Akuba," Esme continued.
"And the pocket," added April.

"And we found the tooth . . ."

"And left the coin . . ."
"And whispered in her ear . . ."
"And got out . . ."

"Just before they got in the taxi."

"OH!" said Grandma.

"Makes me nervous just thinking about it.
  Let's get you home."

Grandad was still reading from
A Poem for Every Day of the Year,
with Vincent's sweet breath in his ear.

He had read four months in one sitting.
"Don't this just beat it all," he said as Grandma,
the girls, and Ariel flew back over the fence.

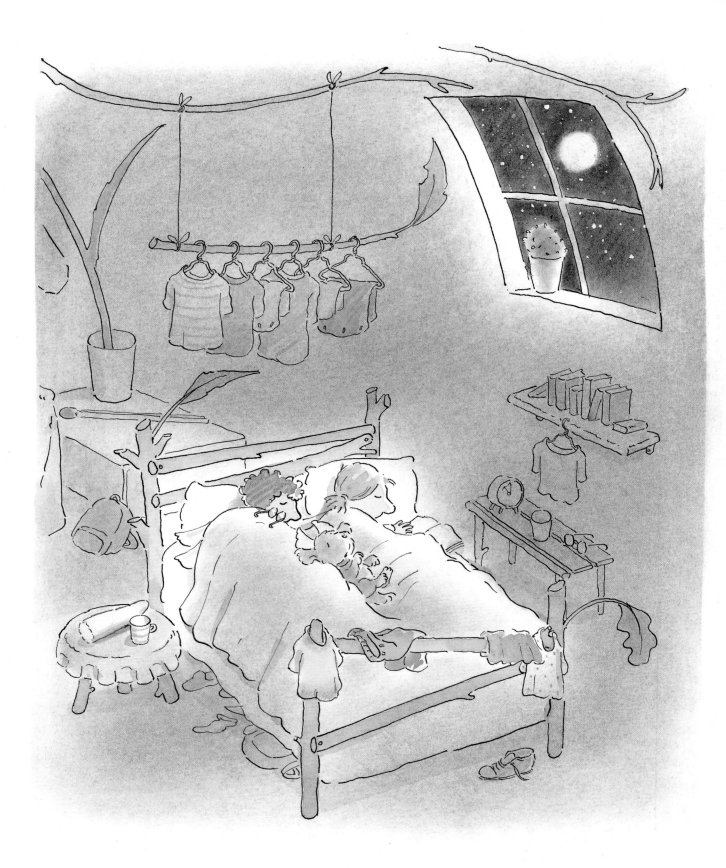

That night a full moon shone through the window of
the teapot home. April and Esme slept in a feather bed,
the baby tooth safe beside them.

Far across the city, the same moon shone on Akuba.
Her tooth now gone, a small coin she found in her
pocket now lay on her bedside table.
And she can't quite remember how it got there.

The moon lay trapped for just a
moment in Grandma's gift.
The first tiny frog had come out of the water,
and the sound of its croak carried faintly up
over the silent airport and
out into the night.